LIB. POE

Mad World

Selected by
Helen Cook
and
Morag Styles

Illustrated by
Caroline Holden

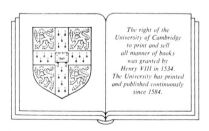

The right of the
University of Cambridge
to print and sell
all manner of books
was granted by
Henry VIII in 1534.
The University has printed
and published continuously
since 1584.

Cambridge University Press

Cambridge
New York   Port Chester
Melbourne   Sydney

Published by the Press Syndicate of the University of Cambridge
The Pitt Building, Trumpington Street, Cambridge CB2 1RP
40 West 20th Street, New York, NY 10011-4211, USA
10 Stamford Road, Oakleigh, Melbourne 3166, Australia

This selection © Cambridge University Press 1991

Illustrations © Caroline Holden 1991

Project editor: Claire Llewellyn

First published 1991

Printed in Great Britain at the University Press, Cambridge

British Library cataloguing in publication data
It's a Mad, Mad, World.
1. Poetry – Anthologies
I. Cook, Helen 1954–   II. Styles, Morag   III. Series
808.81

ISBN 0 521 39958 0

Acknowledgements

'Recipe' from *Selected Poems of Guillevic*, translated by T Savory, Penguin, 1974, from the original 'Recette' from *Avec* by Eugène Guillevic © Éditions Gallimard 1966; 'A Bush-warbler' from *The Narrow Road to the Deep North and Other Travel Sketches* by Basho, translated by Nobuyuki Yuasa (Penguin Classics 1966), copyright © Nobuyuki Yuasa 1966, reproduced by permission of Penguin Books Ltd; 'Snail' by Kobayashi Issa and 'Wild Geese' from *The Penguin Book of Japanese Verse*, translated by Geoffrey Bownas and Anthony Thwaite (Penguin Books, 1964) copyright © Geoffrey Bownas and Anthony Thwaite, 1964; 'Caterpillar's Lullaby' from *Dragon Night* by Jane Yolen, Methuen Children's Books. Reprinted by permission of Curtis Brown Ltd. Copyright © 1980 by Jane Yolen; 'Leaf-eater' by Thomas Kinsella from *The Faber Book of Irish Poetry*, edited by Pasul Muldoon, Faber & Faber Ltd, reprinted by permission of the author; 'The Fly' reprinted by permission of Faber & Faber Ltd from *What is the Truth?* by Ted Hughes; 'How Everything Happens' by May Swenson, copyright © 1969 and used with permission of the Literary Estate of May Swenson; 'Sir Henry Morgan's Song' from *The New Divan* by Edwin Morgan, Carcanet Press Ltd; Valerie Bloom for 'Sun a-Shine, Rain a-Fall'; 'Rain and Sun' from *Rain Falling, Sun Shining* by Odette Thomas, Bogle-L'Ouverture Publications Ltd, 1975; 'Autumn' reprinted by permission of Bloodaxe Books Ltd, from *Poems: Before and After* by Miroslav Holub (Bloodaxe Books, 1990); 'Late Autumn Poem' from *Sky in the Pie* by Roger McGough, reprinted by permission of the Peters, Fraser and Dunlop Group Ltd; 'Its Winter, it's Winter' by Kit Wright, from *Hot Dog and Other Poems* by Kit Wright (Kestrel, 1981) copyright © Kit Wright 1981; 'Reindeer Report' by U A Fanthorpe from *Poems for Christmas*, Peterloo Poets, 1981; 'Nothingmas Day' from *Nothingmas Day* by Adrian Mitchell, Allison and Busby, 1984; 'Cowboy Movies' by John Agard from *Ten Golden Years*, Published by Walker Books Ltd 1989, by kind permission of John Agard, c/o Caroline Sheldon Literary Agency; 'A Child is Singing' from *Poems* by Adrian Mitchell, Jonathan Cape, 1964; 'The Fish are All Sick' from *Selected Poems: 1956–86* by Anne Stevenson, Oxford University Press, 1987, reprinted by permission of Oxford University Press; Carol Ann Duffy for 'Nursery Rhyme'; 'Percy Pot-Shot' copyright © Richard Edwards, 1988, reproduced from *A Mouse in My Roof* by kind permission of Orchard Books, 96 Leonard Street, London EC2A 4RH; 'Extinction Day' reprinted by permission of Pavilion Books from *The Curse of the Vampire's Socks* by Terry Jones.

Every effort has been made to reach copyright holders; the publishers would be glad to hear from anyone whose rights they have unknowingly infringed.

Contents

Recipe 5
Guillevic

Bush-warbler 6
Matsuo Basho

Snail 6
Kobayashi Issa

Wild Geese 7
Traditional, Japan

Caterpillar's Lullaby 8
Jane Yolen

Leaf-eater 9
Thomas Kinsella

The Fly 10
Ted Hughes

How Everything Happens 12
May Swenson

Sir Henry Morgan's Song 14
Edwin Morgan

Sun a-Shine, Rain a-Fall 15
Valerie Bloom

Rain and Sun 15
Odette Thomas

Autumn 16
Miroslav Holub

Late Autumn Poem 17
Roger McGough

It's Winter, it's Winter 18
Kit Wright

'Twas Midnight 19
Anon

Kid Stuff 20
Frank Horne

Reindeer Report 21
U A Fanthorpe

Nothingmas Day 22
Adrian Mitchell

Cowboy Movies 24
John Agard

They Hang the Man 25
Traditional, England

A Child is Singing 26
Adrian Mitchell

The Fish are All Sick 27
Anne Stevenson

Nursery Rhyme 28
Carol Ann Duffy

Percy Pot-Shot 30
Richard Edwards

Extinction Day 32
Terry Jones

Recipe

Take a roof of old tiles
shortly after midday.

Place all beside
a full-grown linden
stirred by the wind.

Put over them
a blue sky washed
by some white clouds.

Leave them alone.
Look at them.

Guillevic

Bush-warbler

A bush-warbler
Coming to the verandah-edge,
Left its droppings
On the rice-cakes.

Matsuo Basho

Snail

Slowly, slowly climb
Up and up Mount Fiji,
O snail.

Kobayashi Issa

Wild Geese

Beating their wings
Against the white clouds
You can count each one
Of the wild geese flying:
Moon, an autumn night.

    Traditional, Japan

Caterpillar's Lullaby

Your sleep will be
a lifetime
and all your dreams
rainbows.
Close your eyes
and spin yourself
a fairy tale:
Sleeping Ugly,
Waking Beauty.

Jane Yolen

Leaf-eater

On a shrub in the heart of the garden,
On an outer leaf, a grub twists
Half its body, a tendril,
This way and that in blind
Space: no leaf or twig
Anywhere in reach; then gropes
Back on itself and begins
To eat its own leaf.

Thomas Kinsella

The Fly

The Fly
Is the Sanitary Inspector. He detects every speck
With his Geiger counter.
Detects it, then inspects it
Through his multiple spectacles. You see him everywhere
Bent over his microscope.

He costs nothing, needs no special attention,
Just gets on with the job, totting up the dirt.

All he needs is a lick of sugar
Maybe a dab of meat –
Which is fuel for his apparatus.
We never miss what he asks for. He can manage
With so little you can't even tell
Whether he's taken it.

In his black boiler suit, with his gas-mask,
His oxygen pack,
His crampons,
He can get anywhere, explore any wreckage,
Find the lost –

Whatever dies – just leave it to him.
He'll move in
With his team of gentle undertakers,
In their pneumatic protective clothing, afraid of nothing,
Little white Michelin men,

They hoover up the rot, the stink, and the goo.
He'll leave you the bones and the feathers – souvenirs
Dry-clean as dead sticks in the summer dust.

Panicky people misunderstand him –
Blitz at him with nerve-gas puff-guns,
Blot him up with swatters.

He knows he gets filthy.
He knows his job is dangerous, wading in the drains
Under cows' tails, in pigs' eye-corners
And between the leaky broken toes
Of the farm buildings –
He too has to cope with the microbes.
He too wishes he had some other job.

But this is his duty.
Just let him be. Let him rest on the wall there,
Scrubbing the back of his neck. This is his rest-minute.

Once he's clean, he's a gem.

A freshly barbered sultan, royally armoured
In dusky rainbow metals.

A knight on a dark horse.

Ted Hughes

How Everything Happens
(BASED ON A STUDY OF THE WAVE)

                                                     happen.
                                              to
                                         up
                                stacking
                            is
                     something

When nothing is happening

When it happens
              something
                    pulls
                        back
                          not
                            to
                              happen.

When   has happened.
     pulling back   stacking up
           happens

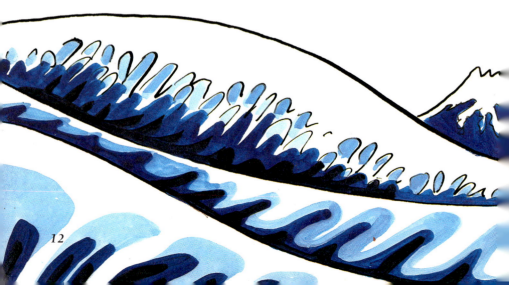

```
              has happened                                    stacks up.
When it              something                      nothing
                                   pulls back while

Then nothing is happening.
                                         happens.
                                   and
                           forward
                     pushes
                 up
              stacks
       something
Then
```

May Swenson

Sir Henry Morgan's Song

we came to the boat and blew the horn
we blew the boom and came to the island
we came the innocent and cut the cackle
we cut the tackle and stripped the bosun
we stripped the brandy and shaved the parrot
we shaved the part and shut the trap
we shut the shroud and bent the log
we bent the ocean and swung the lead
we swung the lumber and blued the lamp
we blued the thunder and crawled the crazes
we crawled Mither Carey and came to St Elmo
we came to the Horn and blew the boat

Edwin Morgan

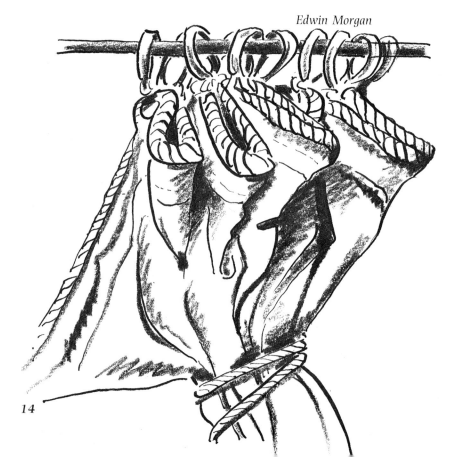

Sun a-Shine, Rain a-Fall

Sun a-shine an' rain a-fall,
The Devil an' him wife cyan 'gree at all,
The two o' them want one fish-head,
The Devil; call him wife bonehead,
She hiss her teeth, call him cock-eye,
Greedy, worthless an' workshy,
While them busy callin' name,
The puss walk in, sey is a shame
To see a nice fish go to was'e,
Lef' with a big grin 'pon him face.

Valerie Bloom

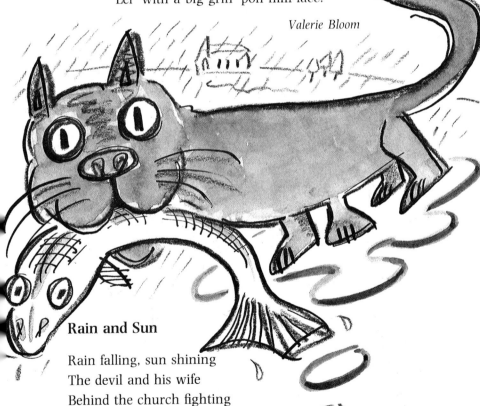

Rain and Sun

Rain falling, sun shining
The devil and his wife
Behind the church fighting

Odette Thomas

Autumn

And it is all over.

No more sweetpeas,
no more wide-eyed bunnies
dropping from the sky.

Only
a reddish boniness
under the sun of hoar frost,
a thievish fog,
an insipid solution of love,
                  hate
                  and craving.

But next year
larches will try
to make the land full of larches again
and larks will try
to make the land full of larks.

And thrushes will try
to make all the trees sing,
and goldfinches will try
to make all the grass golden,

and burying beetles
with their creaky love will try
to make all the corpses
rise from the dead,

Amen.

                      Miroslav Holub

Late Autumn Poem

birdless, and
almost bared,
Trees,
twigs chattering,
  squeeze the last drops
    out of the sun
      and rub them
        deep into parts
          only trees know about.

Roger McGough

It's Winter, it's Winter

It's winter, it's winter, it's wonderful winter,
When everyone lounges around in the sun!

It's winter, it's winter, it's wonderful winter,
When everyone's brown like a steak overdone!

It's winter, it's winter, it's wonderful winter,
It's swimming and surfing and hunting for conkers!

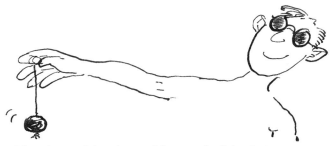

It's winter, it's winter, it's wonderful winter,
And I am completely and utterly bonkers!

Kit Wright

'Twas Midnight

'Twas midnight on the ocean,
Not a streetcar was in sight,
The sun was shining brightly,
For it rained all day that night.
'Twas a summer day in winter
And snow was raining fast
As a barefoot boy with shoes on
Stood sitting on the grass.

Anon

Kid Stuff

The wise guys
tell me
that Christmas
is Kid Stuff . . .
Maybe they've got
something there –
Two thousand years ago
three wise guys
chased a star
across a continent
to bring
frankincense and myrrh
to a Kid
born in a manger
with an idea in his head . . .
And as the bombs
crash
all over the world today
the real wise guys know
that we've all got to go
chasing stars
again
in the hope
that we can get back
some of that
Kid Stuff
born two thousand years ago.

Frank Horne

Reindeer Report

Chimneys: colder.
Flightpaths: busier.
Driver: Christmas (F)
Still baffled by postcodes.

Children: more
And stay up later.
Presents: heavier.
Pay: frozen.

Mission in spite
Of all this
Accomplished:

MERRY CHRISTMAS

U A Fanthorpe

Nothingmas Day

No it wasn't.
It was Nothingmas Eve and all the children in Notown were not tingling with excitement as they lay unawake in their heaps.
D
  o
    w
      n
        s
          t
            a
              i
                r
                  s their parents were busily not placing the last crackermugs, glimmerslips and sweetlumps on the Nothingmas Tree.

Hey! But what was that invisible trail of chummy sparks or vaulting stars across the sky
    Father Nothingmas – drawn by 18 or 21 rainmaidens!
    Father Nothingmas – his sackbut bulging with air!
    Father Nothingmas – was not on his way!
(From the streets of the snowless town came the quiet of unsung carols and the merry silence of the steeple bell.)

Next morning the children did not fountain out of bed with cries of WHOOPERATION! They picked up their Nothingmas Stockings and with traditional quiperamas such as: 'Look what I haven't got! It's just what I didn't want!' pulled their stockings on their ordinary legs.

For breakfast they ate – breakfast.

After woods they all avoided the Nothingmas Tree, where Daddy, his face failing to beam like a leaky torch, was not distributing gemgames, sodaguns, golly-trolleys, jars of humdrums and packets of slubberated croakers.

Off, off, off went the children to school, soaking each other with no howls of 'Merry Nothingmas and a Happy No Year!', and not pulping each other with no-balls.

At school Miss Whatnot taught them how to write No Thank You Letters.

Home they burrowed for Nothingmas Dinner.
The table was not groaning under all manner of
    NO TURKEY
    NO SPICED HAM
    NO SPROUTS
    NO CRANBERRY JELLYSAUCE
    NO NOT NOWT
There was not one (1) shoot of glee as the Nothingmas Pudding, unlit, was not brought in. Mince pies were not available, nor was there any demand for them.

Then, as another Nothingmas clobbered to a close, they all haggled off to bed where they slept happily never after.

and that is not the end of the story . . . .

Adrian Mitchell

Cowboy Movies

On cowboy movies
 they show you Indians as baddies
 and cowboys as goodies

but think again please;

who disturb de dreams
 of de sleeping wigwam
  who come with de guns
   going blam blam blam?

Think again please.

John Agard

They Hang the Man

They hang the man and beat the woman
Who steal the goose from off the common
But let the greater villain loose
Who stole the common from the goose.

Traditional, England

A Child is Singing

A child is singing
And nobody listening
But the child who is singing:

Bulldozers grab the earth and shower it.
The house is on fire.
Gardeners wet the earth and flower it.
The house is on fire,
The houses are on fire.
Fetch the fire engine, the fire engine's on fire.
We will have to hide in a hole.
We will burn slow like coal.
All the people are on fire.

And a child is singing
And nobody listening
But the child who is singing.

Adrian Mitchell

The Fish are All Sick

The fish are all sick, the great whales dead,
The villages stranded in stone on the coast,
Ornamental, like pearls on the fringe of a coat.
Sea men, who knew what the ocean did,
Turned their low houses away from the surf.
But new men who come to be rural and safe
Add big glass views and begonia beds.
Water keeps to itself.
White lip after lip
Curls to a close on the littered beach.
Something is sicker and blacker than fish.
And closing its grip, and closing its grip.

Anne Stevenson

Nursery Rhyme

What do we use to wash our hair?
We use shampoo to wash our hair.
It's tested scientifically for damage to the eyes
by scientists who, in such matters, are acknowledged
to be wise.
Shampoo. Wash hair. Nice, clean habit.
Go to sleep now, darling.
It doesn't hurt the rabbit.

What makes lather in the bath tub?
Soap makes lather in the bath tub.
Rub-a-dub till bubbles bob along the rubber ducks race!
But don't get any in your mouth because soap has a
nasty taste.
Bath time. Slippy soap! Can't quite grab it!
Let's get dried now, darling.
It doesn't hurt the rabbit.

What makes us better when we're ill?
Medicine helps us when we're ill.
Years of research helped to develop every pill you take,
Like that one we gave you when you had a
tummy ache.
Cut knee. Antiseptic. Gently dab it.
Kiss you better, darling.
It doesn't hurt the rabbit.
It doesn't hurt
It doesn't hurt
It doesn't hurt the rabbit.

Carol Ann Duffy

Percy Pot-Shot

Percy Pot-Shot went out hunting,
Percy Pot-Shot and his gun,
Percy Pot-Shot, such a hot shot,
Shot a sparrow, said 'What fun!'

Percy Pot-Shot shot a blackbird,
Shot a lapwing, shot a duck,
Shot a swan as it rose flapping,
Shot an eagle, said 'What luck!'

Percy Pot-Shot shot a rabbit,
Shot a leaping, gold-eyed hare,
Shot a tiger that lay sleeping,
Shot a rhino, shot a bear.

Percy Pot-Shot, trigger happy,
Shot a fountain, shot a tree,
Shot a river, shot a mountain,
Shot some rainclouds, shot the sea.

Percy Pot-Shot went on hunting,
Percy Pot-Shot and his gun,
Not a lot that he had not shot,
Shot the moon down, shot the sun.

Percy Pot-Shot stood in darkness,
No bird fluttered, no beast stirred,
Percy Pot-Shot knelt and muttered
'God forgive me.' No one heard.

Richard Edwards

Extinction Day

The Dodo and the Barbary Lion,
The Cuban Yellow Bat,
The Atlas Bear, the Quagga and
The Christmas Island Rat,
The Thylacine, the Blue Buck
And the Hau Kuahiwi plant
Have all one thing in common now,
And that is that they aren't.

Give me one good reason why,
I wonder if you can?
The answer's in a single word –
The word is simply: Man.

Extinction Day, Extinction Day,
It isn't all that far away
For many animals and birds.
So let us decimate the herds,
Let's hunt their eggs and spoil their land,
Let's give Extinction a Big Hand,
For when it comes, it's here to stay . . .
Extinction Day! Extinction Day!

Terry Jones